Other books
by Alberto Ríos

TEODORO LUNA'S

TWO
KISSES

W·W·NORTON & COMPANY·NEW YORK·LONDON

TEODORO LUNA'S

TWO
KISSES

POEMS BY ALBERTO RÍOS

Printed in the United States of America

The epigraph on p. 12 is from "Shoreline Horses," in *The Lime Orchard Woman* by Alberto Ríos.

The text of this book is composed in Primer with the display set in Clarendon Condensed. Composition and manufacturing by The Maple-Vail Book Manufacturing Group. Book design by Antonina Krass.

First Edition

Library of Congress Cataloging-in-Publication Data
Ríos, Alberto.
     Teodoro Luna's two kisses : poems / Alberto Ríos.
        p.   cm.
     I. Title.
   PS3568.I587T4   1990b
   811'.54—dc20   90–38621
   ISBN 0-393-02868-2

W.W. Norton & Company, Inc., 500 Fifth Avenue, New York, N.Y. 10110
W.W. Norton & Company, Ltd., 37 Great Russell Street, London WC1B 3NU

1 2 3 4 5 6 7 8 9 0

To my family, all of you,
So many places,
These recent years, so much coming
And going.

A Note about Loteria

The images on the dust cover of this book are adapted from the game called Loteria. My family remembers playing Loteria as children in Mexico, at least as far back as the twenties, and they're certain it existed before that. The game is like Bingo, but all of the squares are representations—visual icons—of the ordinary: the ladder, the moon, the hand, and so on. Because the images were labeled underneath and the game was brightly printed, Loteria functioned as a method of teaching reading and colors, as well as being an entertainment.

In other versions, there are folk sayings relevant to the images on the backs of the cards. On "La Pera," the Pear, for example, the card reads: "El que espera/desespera." The person who waits/despairs. The word "pear" suffers in translation, appearing in English as "despair." In that moment of survival beyond the borders of language and landscape, and in the way the word does change, much of this book resides.

Contents

Three

The following poems first appeared in these journals and anthologies:

American Poetry Review: "The Good Lunch of Oceans," "What Is Quiet
    in the Spelling of Wednesday."
Ironwood: "The Death of Anselmo Luna," "Teodoro Luna's Two Kisses."
Journal of Ethnic Studies: "Animals and the Noon Street," "How She
    Finds Me."
Kenyon Review: "Mexico, from the Four Last Letters," "Indentations
    in the Sugar."
Manoa: "Hers Is the Noise, Also, of the Dogs Asleep and in Dream."
The New Yorker: "The Influenzas," "Mr. Luna in the Afternoon."
New England Review and Bread Loaf Quarterly: "Passing Late in the Day's
    Afternoon a History," "Half Hour of August."
The Paris Review: "Mr. Luna in History."
Ploughshares: "Marvella, for Borrowing," "Teodoro Luna's Old Joke."
Prairie Schooner: "Leaving Off."
Willow Springs: "Lost on September Trail, 1976," "The Sea by Holding."

Firewheel Press originally printed "Not Shaving on Some Days" as a
    broadside.
My thanks also to the Guggenheim Foundation and to Arizona State
    University.

—He had by accident glimpsed,
   He said, *her left breast,*

   The point of it
   On the inside of the green blouse

   That shoreline
   Horse of the new world.

PART

ONE

The Used Side of the Sofa

When she walked
She left herself
Where she had been.
Every year that treadled
Asked something of her,
And with every breath
She breathed out more
Than she took in,
And when she walked
She left her footprints,
Then her feet,
As she later could feel
Nothing under her.
When she sat then rose
She left an indentation.
A part of her
Too comfortable,
Not following so easily
The rest of her.
And when enough was gone,
An arm forgotten here,
Or there a leg
Fallen asleep,
We learned to walk
Quickly through her.
We excused ourselves,
Begged her pardon
Those first years,
But then there were
So many of us

And walking so fast,
It was better simply
To say nothing
So that she did not feel
The need to respond.

Hers Is the Noise, Also, of the
Dogs Asleep and in Dream

Milagros in a moment of weakness
Wished upon her mother
An unkindness, which came to be.

Seeing what she had wrought,
The extreme manner by which her mother
Was taken,

Milagros thought to herself
Just being sad was not reasonable
Enough penance for what she had done.

A sadness was good
Only for making more of the eyes
Than is there,

For the geometric making
Of breaths longer and then longer
Until just breathing is everything.

This was the taste
Impossible things had.
But Milagros wanted

Something even more difficult
Than the taste of a life
Which cannot be lived.

With resolve to go farther,
And to even up accounts
With her mother,

Milagros on purpose
Got herself lost
And turned around in her sadness.

She took care to make
Only as many fires
Along the trail of her insides

As would sustain
The making of her food,
Which was a mystery.

The doctors to their credit
Recognized her condition.
They provided for Milagros

A brace specially made
To keep her from looking up,
A variation of that

Used on starbucks,
Those horses of God
That despair.

Anselmo's Moment with God

Anselmo in a fit of pique
Over a spatula he could not find
As the eggs were burning
And as he did not yet have the services
Of the housekeeper Mrs. M.
He would have in later years,
Renounced his love of God
And of the world, right there.

He threw the drawer of utensils to the ground
And let the eggs burn dry
Until they gave texture to
And became part of the black iron pan itself.
Every day for the rest of his life
He remembered himself that moment—
Himself but not the event:
His spatula became through the years
The Hand of God.

Of God's smell
He could not be certain:
Only that the burning of candles
Had for him a certain urgency.

The Death of Anselmo Luna

Since he was the priest,
No one could say for certain about Anselmo Luna.
What began as a lark
One slow afternoon of interminable chores
Regarding candles and residue on the walls,
Became his drawings:
First of the saints,
Then the twelve Stations of the Cross,
The sketches of simpler remembrances.
All of these chiaroscuros he made
In and from the soot on the walls of this church,
A work that moved into years
And which finally filled his life.
What began as a lark became the seed
Of his miracle, a simple
Moving of a finger along a pillar
Just to see, was there enough
To require cleansing,
This test also used on parked cars,
A line spelling *wash me* in the soil of a window.
He died while perched on a ladder
High behind the altar, underneath
The fine woodwork: that moment
As he fell, and as he made a mark
Not unlike a moustache
Where none should have been,

He died already partway
Toward heaven. It was said
His soul took the advantage,
Leaping out from his body
Right there, stepping from his ribs
As he had stepped
On the rungs of the ladder.
It was a strong soul, muscular,
On account of his years of devoted effort,
And it knew like an animal what to do
When the moment came.

Indentations in the Sugar

As they have no difficulty with walls,
Neither do they have the services of a table,
And so the dead do not stay
Longer than twenty minutes,
The time it takes to make coffee
Mid-morning.
Sometimes we find a broken cup,
And we remember them, through the years
Their eyeglasses growing thicker.
But theirs was a preparation for the long
Look from there to here,
So that small things like cups
Up close are hard to handle.
And they do look,
Our features bending and parting
In the fat manner of that circus
Mirror in front of which we all stood
In our turn, making two-foot mouths.
Sometimes the glasses are not thick enough
So that they walk through us
To get to the other side of the kitchen,
Imagining they have a small need
Putting a hand through ours
Reaching for a stirring spoon.
For us it is bursitis or the thrill
Feel of coolness.

Their twenty-minute visits are finally
A courtesy of the centuries,
And they are impatient to go.
They shake their heads about things.
It's this kitchen, they say;
          The spoons are not good spoons.
We don't hear them.
It is the open window.

The Influenzas

The last of the epidemics bore him
Specially away, a favorite
Son of their group
In that he had taken such care with them,
Always being sick;
The illnesses came as a knock
Regular at the door,
And his invitation
Which might have seemed tired from another—
Please come in—
Was full of the ready enthusiasm
For which he was known in all things,
And always the wink of mischief in melodrama:
Always the big show
Hunching his shoulders
That his wife should not see.
Keeping him quiet and in socks, illness
And its children over the years
Made a second home here,
In him,
At the dinner table
Behind his eyes, sitting
In the most comfortable chair
This with-drawing room in his face had to offer,
Filled drinks always in hand.
This man was a comfort in his manners—
Even disease could see this,
So that when he left he went
Voluntarily, all intentions honest:
Out there tonight the party for him was to be

Very good, and to be there without him now
Would be unbearable.
With his hat, his heavy coat,
Walking that way he walked
When he was quiet in his socks,
Hunching his shoulders so that his wife
Again should not see
Him, with his friends he went drinking
The hundred good glasses of very cold beer.

The Good Lunch of Oceans

I ate with my father
The avocado
And thought without telling him
The skin of a sidewalk
Dirty with stones. It is the
Harbor line of Thrill
And the swim inside.
Scrotum skin,
I could not tell him.
How its feel was of sutures
Holding the body together
At its very base.
        Green meat,
Feel of sand completely
Wet, a fragile
Lip meat, mouth
Meat of dreams
Two places on her body.
        Green in a garden
Of celeries and the lost
Cat-eye marble
That won me everything.
Old Chevrolet paint, green
Virgin of Guadalupe,
That famous painting
The color of the Thirties,
From which deep orange
Has also survived. Green
That used to be green.

Failed ocarina
Little bear
Shape of an ocean,
I eat our avocado
With my father, play
For its music
In my mouth.

Fixing Tires

Your rough hands, pins:
On me they make
The tin rasp my father used
Patching the bad
Tires of the round-back
Chevy, that fast, hard,
Repeat scrape making
Everything smooth
By its unevenness,
Smooth for the honey
Solvent to which we lit
A match and watched
It burn,
That fire making a seal
Sticky and, we could see,
Firm. This skin
You show me now,
The skin thrilling makes,
Up against my cheek,
This rubbing
Along all my lips,
It is the rasp
And strong enough.

How She Finds Me

She has very long lips.
She calls me that way
        With her mouth
The way I remember it
Touching mine, moving
Through the valleys
Toward my fingers,
Into them

And her eyes, too:
Long, or big,
They can see me,
Have looked long
Into the frank jet of dream

        How with the dancers
        I can only say yes
        Again, To the tango
        And the hands The way their hands
                With the quiet and loud
        The yes and the no Their starting and stopping,
        For me, say I will

There is room here for everything
Which cannot be said.
That I have dreamed
The inside of the outside.

Not Shaving on Some Days

Going to work or returning
The same way home
The buildings are still
Written on by boys.
The girl who considers herself,
They say on the walls, a prize
Is most famous here
Her parts described and drawn
In generous scale
Most to least important
In the informative manner
City newspapers engage.
I have been immune
But a day off from work comes.
The immediate gristle on the face
That holds me
Holds on these same days
The things all misplaced around me,
Putting lines in my hands,
Red in my eyes and on my breath.
Today mine is a face remarkably like
Drawn with pin-dotted beard
The face of a bad man
In a comic book.
I am a different man on these days.
A man whose beard he can see
Is that dirty workman's rasp,

A thousand small explosions,
An offering of dirty fingers
Out and moving.
Sometimes, and sometimes it is
The garden at its moment.

What a Boy Can Do

February, and the wind has begun
Milk cartons moving along the curb,
An occasional wrapper, Baby Ruth.

The young tree bends in a hoeing.
Cirrus clouds, sparrows, jet trailings:
Each puts a line on the sky. February

Kites, too, their shapes: the way three
Boys have taken their baseball fields
Into the air, flying them on strings.

When I flew my kite I shouted, louder,
Anything, strong, boy wild and rocks:
February was here. I was helping.

Leaving Off

Eight wrens
Looking like fists
Drop, these stones
A boy might throw.
Landing without sounds
With only the small orchid
Hitting makes
On the skin of a lake,
They move neatly
Toward their food. A man
Stands erect, his back
An Eiffel line,
Stops the picking of cold season
Fruit from the trees.
He has heard the wrens anyway
Knows a silence like theirs
Is the noise of wrens
Going somewhere.
They have come from the air
Up with the leaves, bits, kites
The geese and day stars
A floating horizon.
The wrens finish and go
Leaving off this way
One winter, one year.

Lost on September Trail, 1976

Evening Eight

Our shoes were not our shoes
In the evening, not the shoes
With the morning we had put on.
And so our steps were not our steps,
And where we went we did not go.
We did not enter the night
Did not eat as our dinner
Our new world dinner
A black white as straws
Sipped through on those high school dates
Four shoes touching underneath
The table, the underside
Of the table, the stuff and gum and glue.
We did not enter the thought
Of that night
Whose hands were big
Wanting to grasp anything hard.
There was no ease in them.
We did not enter
The skin of those bodies
Loving them for what they wanted.
We did not talk,
Did not touch our tongues
To our tongues
In a toast of what we remembered
Having wanted,
Having not had, until now.
Our evenings were not our days:

They were always somewhere else
Farther than the rim of the mountains
And the trail and the trees and the wind.

Day Three

We have packed too much for camping,
The sheer joke of a watermelon
Lost now
So that lunch is a red thing
But good
Finally and exhausted.
Lunch all over our faces,
What is disagreeable
Spit out against the sky,
The lunch of lunches
We would not have again.

Day Nine

No words
But in the will of the walking.
This language.

Evening Two

All the stories of all the times
Everything happened to each of us,

Each one old and new
At the same time,
Back to back in the same words
Words opposite not in meaning
But in time, the impossibility,
The magic-like wateriness in the air
Underneath our laughing.
Laughing so hard we are crying,
Opposites again.
And ourselves, too:
The same exactly but different.
The way yes and no fit on this line.

That we are older and were younger, too;
Looking at those photographs,
That we can be two places at once,
Can remember, can smell
What in each of them is there.

Day Five

Today rain, and at first
We liked it, the slow sing of its starting.
But it turned to fingers
Irritating, that way someone angry pokes
Another person's chest
Who does not like it
Does not like it, not at all.
      Under the shirt
      A body does not forget
      So fast, its throbbing first
      Then its hurt colors,
      A small yellow, a purpling.

A small vomiting,
A swelled throat.
And the rain made us heavier, us slower.
Instead of reaching the campsite
We had to accept the gift
Odd trees held out to us.
Under them, still light in the distance,
We watched the day,
Saw how it was somewhere else, again.
Saw that night was impatient for us,
Opening a mouth over everything.

Evening Nine

Orion, and Rigel, the Milky Way,
The illumined black,
The difficulty of the Little Dipper:
We can only talk about the stars
Because it is a distance familiar.

PART

TWO

Marvella, for Borrowing

1.

Lately in her full arms
I had felt the things
That would not go, the hands:
She had gathered to herself
Some part of all of the fingers
Of all of the men who had
Touched her there, Florencio,
His broad fingers like past winter gloves,
Caetano who was matches,
César, who could only see
By his fingers, and how hard
He had looked, all the many hours
For a finger to be an eye,
And then the sadness.

2.

Lately in her arms
The fullness was everything,
All of those fingers
All over me, at first
Feeling like desire.
But it was with those vast arms
As well that she flew,
The way the fingers of a man
Cannot stop, and so they suspended her
Better than the new engines.
I have seen her hovering

With those monstrous arms
At the window, I have seen her
Though I have tried
To shield my eyes:
Too quickly I made the gesture
In the old way
As if I myself still had hands.

3.

And this is just one thing,
Because the men touched her with everything.
And their eyes, these were the heaviest
Of all she was made to carry,
The eyes and what those eyes
Desired to see on her,
So that under her clothes
Through the years she grew
Half-wings, the small tail with feathers,
Breasts as big as elephant buttocks.

4.

And the men grew thinner
Because they looked too hard,
And each long whistle they made
Rudely was one inch too much of the rooster soul.
Those noises became indentations under clothes,
Spaces in place of protrusions;
Marvella in her turn
Became with so many appendages
A hundred men.
I watched her in the window suspended,
And then flying, with her fat and old arms

And her half-wings,
Taking me with her as well, everything
Save the kindness of having left
In memory of a particular morning
These eyes and this mouth.

Mr. Luna in the Afternoon

He could not say that he prayed
Except in that he was often happy,
Prayer being resident there.

His dream was the same.
A Greek morning
Warm, foreign, sheep noises and flowers,
Waking to walls
Unsound, but doing their job
Regardless of the rules
For walls.

She put her body in his mouth.
Some things persist, without
Written instruction. He knew
What to do.
This was not the hard bosom
Of a small wife, but he knew
What to do, his mouth
As if it held a saltine.

He drank in long
The afternoons of winter
Not winter anymore.

Until her eyes were anti-sparks
And her arms,
Her thousand arms,
You know them,
Those pecan trees
Along the orchard road.

Mr. Luna and History

There are many facts in the world.
Most are passengers, but some
Drive the car.
The boy king Tutankhamen caused to be made
For himself the first bed.
In 1340, Thomas Blanket was said to have had
A refinement.
And in 1932, as schoolchildren know,
Teodoro Luna, president of all that had come before,
Invented the making of love.

So went the old joke,
Which was funny but not untrue.
There was talk after his death of a statue,
But the thought of it was enough,
Pigeons landing not on his head or arms,
But rather on his fame,
Two dozen of them.

Some mouths have the custom of food,
Some of words. Most go with food.
Mr. Luna's mouth had the habit of women.

In his later years his wife thought him
Speaking in his sleep,
But that was not it,
His mouth moving sometimes like a yawn,
Sometimes like a fish.

It is said
A perfect diamond is invisible in water.
How Mr. Luna died is not known,
Nor what happened to his body.
It is said he gave some of himself each time,
From the inside and the out,
Awake but also in dream.
It is said he became a thousand women.

Waiting for My Mother

1.

    Well I'll wait, it's no bother.
She picked up a small book
To fan from herself some of the weather
She had brought in on her back.
I thought to leave her sitting
Alone for a moment in the kitchen,
But knew better about manners.
This was the small Doña Carolina,
A woman who had never begun or ended
A conversation, trapped
Always in the middle,
And therefore famous in her cage
Like those capuchin monkeys that time.

2.

Today her first words sounded as if to be
Something of a beginning,
But I was still young.
She looked at the book with which she fanned:
    A, she said, they said to her
When she still wore her first braids,
Had I heard this too?
The letter *A* stood for Apples.
Ah. As if a little letter could make it so—
Write *A* and *sas!* Apples.
As if any of us had seen apples that summer.

3.

I'm not a stupid woman.
They didn't know it, but I could read
All right, I knew what spelled what.
A was apples only in the way
Two breasts become hard
When there's nothing.
Like that, A was everywhere,
But it was mostly my comadre, Luisa.
A was her picture.

4.

The way letters of the alphabet
Have always been
Pictures: Luisa's two legs, her body folded
Over them in a pool.

> Sometimes I see A as the shape of a man,
> One of the men who pushed our door,
> The peak, his back, the line
> His belt.

5.

B, should you lie it on its side
To see it better? Those testicles
Searching for their body.
Before, we were not allowed to say that word.
But now they're everywhere.

Well, when we are asked, we tell the kids
They're sparrow eggs,
Hanging in the trees.

6.

C is how a man begs
For whatever is left.
And the letter *Ch* is the addition of a small chair
From which his interrogators
Permit him to fall.

>   *Can't you imagine it?*
>   *The oldest lines in the world:*
>   *Don Julio, my friend,*
>   *You must tell us what you know.*

7.

From *C* to *D*, from round back to straight—
Do you see, how the body stiffens
Its spine at the snap of a rod across it,
The back of Don Julio made to stand
By the speeded elbow
A hard man always uses first.

8.

E. This is the famous map
Showing how from a line of men
Three broke forward, west to east
Fast across the field.
And then *F*.
This is a second map, of Don Julio's
Fall to the first rounds.

When I tell the truth, this is not
A map. It is a photograph,
See? But you knew, of Don Julio himself
And of how he was made to lose his feet.

9.

Did you know him, she asks, my husband?
The small Doña Carolina sat
Fanning herself again
Her hair back a little in the breeze.
By this act and in repose
I watch her own body,
How it makes with its bones
A letter I too can hear.

The Sea by Holding

Each wave in, the end of a line:
The sea in making them both shoreworthy
Makes *can* and *wrapper* rhyme;
Draws one more song
From the dead bird
In showing it as a mismatched
Contraption pushed up
Past the last lick of the waterlines—
The song of the dead birds:
It is the noise we
Make, faced
Suddenly by one.
  Take this
We are told, as if cupping a shell
Hard to our good, telephone ear:
   Anyway I'm glad you came.
   I found this
   Sometime last week.
   It's not, well you know, mine
   And I need someone
   To return it
   As surely in its absence
   Someone must be looking,
   A blue thing like this,
   Perhaps some reward . . .
We turn our eyes
And the bird stops its song,
As that shell taken from the ear
Releases us.
A shell to the ear,

This bird to the eyes.
We will always look away,
This way
Daring what rhymes us
With the holdings of the sea.

Mexico, from the Four Last Letters

Some stories arrive as the
mysterious tintype of a woman, removed from a box after years.
Certainly she is a relative, but no one can say who
with clarity any longer.

1.

We dream together
The bad thing
We do not tell him
In our letter:
It is about Imuris, next
Fall: his famous
Five horses,
One from which
Steam will rise
For hours
After the accident.
We dream
M. will write us
Saying so.

2.

The famous
Five horses:
After the work of the hay
They become
Five young dogs
In the afternoon,

Going afterward
To an evening of cards.

3.

M. writes
The horses are well.
His daughter from her window
Imagines them
Dolls, she says,
Old Saturnino in a white dress.

4.

It was not
One of the horses
But the girl we saw
In the dream, in the way
She saw the horses.
She was the one
In a white dress,
Steam rising
From her.
He says she had risen
Through the window
Pulled by her eyes
Which were the largest
Part of her
In those days,
Had risen and gone through
The window. She had tried,
He says, to run
The run of the horses.
And something at the sight

Of their twenty legs
Had carried her
A little, lifted her.

5.

M. writes the horses are
Well, but slower
In these days now.
His work is a chore
And the wind
An irritation.
The days have changed.
He says the one horse
Ambrosio will work
Only half-days.
Then he sits down.

What Is Quiet in the
Spelling of Wednesday

Rain but not rain
The way rain had come before
Came through the window
It had broken.

Drops bounced off the sill
Hard and were so fat
They flew back up
Inside, where they reached
In the manner of the trapeze
Man's hands
The ceiling, water
Like the textured stubble
Of some ceilings

Collecting at several points
As if to fall. The droplets
Pulled on themselves.
The ceiling with its own
Hands would not release them,
These hands made
From what must go to ceilings,
The odors of years,

> Old webs, and webs upon them,
> The unclean everything,
> Dreams, what stays
> When one shouts so loud
> Words echo off the walls,

Only halfway coming back,
The rest of the words

Staying, that skin.
The droplets do not finally
Fall, they ride
Everything down from the ceiling,
Gum and mucous strings
To the floor, landing
More than falling,
A thousand on these quick vines
From another world.

The droplets land
In a white shag rug, the one
The dog has chosen for himself,
His hair timbers
To this water.

We cannot see it,
But we step into the wetness
Presuming this water to have come
The regular way, just down
Straight from the window.

And we presume even the window
Has been broken by something else,
A broom handle,
The way it happened twice before.

Teodoro Luna's Two Kisses

Mr. Teodoro Luna in his later years had taken to kissing
His wife
Not so much with his lips as with his brows.
This is not to say he put his forehead
Against her mouth—
Rather, he would lift his eyebrows, once, quickly:
Not so vigorously he might be confused with the villain
Famous in the theaters, but not so little as to be thought
A slight movement, one of accident. This way
He kissed her
Often and quietly, across tables and through doorways,
Sometimes in photographs, and so through the years themselves.
This was his passion, that only she might see. The chance
He might feel some movement on her lips
Toward laughter.

Teodoro Luna's Old Joke

—for Lupita

Teodoro Luna met a woman for whom he cared instantly,
She loved him back,
And together two weeks later they stepped into a marriage
Eighty-three miles long.
It was his little joke, this calling of the years miles,
And she would feign anger
At this man who through the years had earned the right
To call them by any words,
Her man with his one ear now because of war, her Teodoro
With his one arm
The other worn away from milking the many lines of filled cows
And pumping the water.
She could see now in her man in his eyes the second white parts
Of what he was becoming.
First his hair, and his eyes, sometimes his flatfish tongue.
She kept looking,
How he had begun to wither, the wisps of his brows, the white
Lines of saliva,
The white arcs of his nails, his scars, his teeth and his legs,
The foldings of his face.
He was she saw making of himself in time the moth's cocoon,
That he might break from it,
A strong push and strong unfolding first of one new shoulder,
Then of the other.
She would be there to the end, to the minute exactly, dressed
In the red dress ready,
That he would be young enough again for the both of them,
That he might lift her,
The way he had lifted her the first time with his many eyes.

Mr. Luna's Plum Tree

In his pants sometimes he felt
So much of himself he thought
To himself what he could not say out loud:
How he must have been a plum tree
In the other life, full bloom,
A hundred purple, can he say, testicles?
Hung on a trunk wide as a housepainter's
Main brush. Like an appendix, his vestige
Tree limb might have been from another time;
Unlike the appendix, however,
He had through the years found for it
A suitable use.
On these days he thought
As he walked he made the noise of low bells,
Pitched to the sound of extraordinary strain,
As when he with the shoulders of his groin
Moved the Jaramillo piano by himself,
The sound of profound efforts, of thunder
From on top of the earth,
Or a sound from the earth inside itself.
Beyond the joy of its further architecture,
He imagined for a moment a lion's addition,
Its roaring against this renting of the sky,
A gathering of inarticulated operas
With which to make the world,
Noises which are long-hammer sounds
Coming in through the screen door
From somewhere down in the canyon;
Threnody notes from the curious

Workaday song of the world's making,
Thunder, bell, lion, together they made
The sound of a chance groan come up
From the centuries,
A collective remembrance:
An act of love is finally
Not different from the earthquake in jokes:
Did the earth move for you too?
He was a man of the world, so to speak,
And had knowledge of these phrases.
A man of the world
Or a man of the movie theaters.
Sometimes in his pants these plums
And this tree made him laugh hard
Along the sidewalk of the New World.
But wait, he thought,
There are the structures of women,
What of the way they are made?
And how could I have forgotten them.
What does a woman feel
In the pockets of her cotton dress
As it drapes down from along her hips?
For a moment he had owned
The making of the world by himself.
He had something more now
To work out on his walk
Gone mid-morning, toward lunch,
In front of the Jaramillo house famous
For the thousand-pound push,
The thousand-pound baby he might have made
Had his pants fallen
And the instrument's curiously shaped door
Opened.

PART

THREE

Teodoro Luna Confesses After Years to His Brother, Anselmo the Priest, Who Is Required to Understand, But Who Understands Anyway, More Than People Think

I am a slave to the nudity of women.
I do not know with what resolve

I could stand against it, a naked woman
Asking of me anything.

An unclothed woman is sometimes other things.
I see her in a dish of green pears.

Anselmo, do you know what I mean if I say
Without clothes

Her breasts are the two lions
In front of the New York Public Library,

Do you know that postcard of mine?
In those lions there is something

For which I have in exchange
Only sounds. Only my fingers.

I see her everywhere. She is the lions
And the pears, those letters of the alphabet

As children we called dirty, the W,
The Y, the small o.

She is absolutely the wet clothing on the line.
Or, you know, to be more intimate,

May I? The nub, the nose of the pear,
Do you know what I mean? Those parts of the woman

I will call two Spanish dancer hats,
Or rounder sometimes, doughboy helmets from the War.

Sometimes they are flat in the late afternoon
Asleep. Like drawings,

Like a single rock thrown into the lake,
These parts of a woman an imperfect circling

Gyre of lines moving out, beyond the water.
They reach me at the shore, Anselmo.

Without fail, they are stronger,
And they have always been faster than I am.

It's like watching the lassoing man,
The man with the perfectly circling rope,

Pedro Armendariz in the Mexican movies,
Or Will Rogers. Wherever one is from,

Whoever this man is.
And he is always there. Everybody knows one.

He always makes his big lasso, twirling his rope
Around himself and a woman from the audience

Only I am the woman, do you understand, Anselmo?
Caught in the circling rope. I am the woman

And me thinking of a woman
Without clothes

Is that man and that rope
And we are riding on separate horses.

Uncle Christmas

Not more vulgar than any other
Uncle, he knew his place
Among them, but he was the most

Uncle of the uncles,
And when he died
He did it well, filled

With the resonant
Earth-rich failings of his kidneys,
Whiskey and his big life,

Summed up in the same space
His stomach took,
That kindly thing

Which had kept his belt buckle
From harm, which had kept him
From hugging his nieces

The way he wanted.
It hung there.
A cement mixer, mixing

A concrete we could hear inside.
No shirt was adequate.
His one suit coat fit

Like sideburns on a face.
Everything I knew about him
Was stomach,

His hungover days
Pouring gravel
With the highway department

Dressed in hard colored vests
Orange and yellow
As if they were hunters.

These were the fabled
Men who made noise
At women.

He was called "the goat,"
But it was friendly.
No one told us why.

He had a thin moustache
The kind from the movies,
Red skin, black hair

And delicate hands.
The beer went straight to his eyes,
Which were always angel fish

In the back room of a pet shop,
The way you look at them
Moving at soft angles

Through the glass.
I remember his yard and the dog,
His perfect sons

He loved more than his wife.
They could have anything,
And even as a child I understood

This extreme unction at work,
This long dying.
Christ of the beers,

His lesson in how to be the man.
He suffered himself
And was happy.

A Dish of Green Pears

A year
With invisible brushes
Can paint fruit,
Can turn it
To painting on a tablecloth canvas,
Sculpt it with inhuman delicacy
And right choices,
Make rabbits and gasoline
Waves rise from it,
Earmuffs out of pears.
Then a year folds its workplace,
Taking the easel
At the change in fall light.

So too with a man's body left
In service to the skills of this artist.
Or to love, to marriage,
To the intangibles: Famine or desire,
A woman's tongue only once:
The abiding memory of what is possible,
Always Mariquita
The fire and the cloddish itch
Making centuries of literature
And the heart of crime.

Memory is a violence
To the moment now.
It will not leave well enough alone.
Remembrance of a singular lower lip.
Remembrance in its costume of a cruel burr

Under a horse's blanket.
Whoever is important to us now,
They will ask, What's wrong with us,
What's in us making us move.
How many years does it take.

This man's skin is a drum's covering.
A drum skin, smooth on the one side,
An unfinished rot
Of leather drippings
And misalignments underneath.

Animals and the Noon Street

On a Thursday when I was young a man

Wrestled with me. I never forgot
The smell of his arms
On my face, his five arms
Giving me the gift of the animal,
The five faces of the monster animal,
Ice things, things coal,
Cold black nothing, an empty
Big as the night sky when I am standing
On a plain with nothing
To hold me down onto the floor of the planet,
A black that draws in
Aimed down on the smallness of me and pulling up.
All around, even in the day they pretend
Not to be anything, and some people saying
They're just shadows, harmless, don't
Be afraid. But it's the animals
Hiding over there behind everything:
And no one is finally fooled,
No one, not me, no: I know
The animals, and the animals know me.
We are straight that way
With each other about things.

I carry matches to burn

Them with the light. I step on them
When I can, when they stay
Fixed that way they do when they pretend

To be shadows, step on
Their testing cat paws, their whiskers
The shadows parking meters make.
I step on them hard, mash
Them underneath, whistle through
Them—they're afraid of whistling, of wind,
Afraid of sounds that come from inside
People, inside me: they hate
The screams of the parts of them
I have eaten, the parts I have
Trapped inside me. So I am safe
If I am quick enough to shake
My voice like a fist
Inside. To whistle. The animals
They are manageable like that,
By fighting.

Leaving August

Fall impends, a cool
Evening shade and cement
Driveway. The boys
Ride bikes differently
Now and birds look twice
From the eaves. The heat
Is going from this place,
Not fast but with blue hands

And in black shoes.
At night stars
Are stars more,
And the air is a rider
On itself.
Some girls will come back
From the summer all right,
Some the month August

Will have kept too much of,
Taken as a chance confidant,
Summer with its big mouth
And horizon moustache,
Its mouth full of men, its breath
Warm down a still back,
Making a girl shiver
As a woman passes through her

Who is bigger than the skin
This girl has to contain her.
These are the girls more quiet

Than last year, already
Walking ahead on the trail,
Maria-this, Maria-that,
All of them
With the names of saints.

But Fall insists.
Coolness bristles the skin
Sloppy with its hand,
An opposite to the rubbing
Of somebody's arm quickly,
To fire.
I watch the girls I knew
Walking ahead of me.

Sometimes a feeling
Gathers slow, and their walk
Is like a sudden walking of blood
Into a private part,
Not so much then
In need of satisfaction
As, instead, of rectification:
An ocean liner,

It is the small joke,
Too many people gathering
On one side of the ship.
Here is circumstance, not desire.
A suddenness of moment simply felt,
To which one is a party
Anyway, the cold unbloom
Of an old season.

In a Borrowing Time

1.

When she died she did not die,
She had no life to give.
June in her hair and August
In her eyes, she could not keep
Her parts.
What she had, she had to borrow,
What she gave no one could take.
Her life was long
But her legs were short,
And where she went she ran.
Some said she died of the whispers
Small towns sometimes get
Instead of wind
But in truth she had heard
One afternoon cold
At a kitchen table
How a perfect diamond is,
Invisible in water.
She tried to be, but could not.
She was pulled on a Thursday
Hard from the small north river.

2.

But they did not pull all of me
Back, I said, they did not
Bring everything
Into the house. Someone

Slipped eight of my fingers
Into a coat pocket
And forgot.

3.

I could not find the day.
I had lost it as well
Along the cottonwoods and the road,
Left it perhaps
In the other purse
Hung on the back of a brown door
Whose house I could not recall.

4.

I woke in the darkness
When the darkness woke in me.
The juncture was sudden,
The unexpected slip when walking,
A paper cut
In the midst of routine.
Seeing somebody you know in a car
That drives by.

5.

Where the shorelines had grown
Over, onto the river: there
The banks move in waves, Hawaiian
Dancers of the hula
In grass skirts and black hair:
Their hands say something,

But a boat goes by
And I cannot make it out.
I hear only the monkey sounds
Which might be made
Were someone to read
A page typed by hands
Misaligned on a typewriter's keys.
A shoreline against a river
Should have an edge,
I think. Something from childhood
To say what is river,
What is not.

6.

My husband pushed himself into me
And did not come out.
He finished with me and walked away
But I could still feel him, as if
There were two of him this moment,
The man at the mirror and the same man
In me. As he stood at the mirror
I saw that it was possible,
There as he himself looked at another
One of himself.
Now there were three of him,
And I began to think there were more:
Under the bed, catching the hem of my gown,
Pretending to make the noise of red leaves
Outside my small window.
I began to remember an odd reflection of him
Here and there through the years,
In a spoon or in a store window.

I began to think of his shadow
And of his photographs.
I began to think I too must be him.
I began to think he was everywhere
And in everything. I began to think
I could not breathe.
That if I did he would be in me again,
A different way.

7.

I knew his name and could write it
But it was better spelled
By the spent bear-sounds he made
In the moment after his kind of love,
Those noises from the inside
Saying his real
Given and family names.

8.

A big sound likes to stay around in a church
Have coffee
Talk big
But it loves me even more,
It says,
And has come to stay
Pretending to be a comfort.
But a big noise, who can trust it.
Still, I was polite,
And told no one. Where else,
I think, can a big noise go.
I knew its true story,

Shushed out of church
More than once.
To go back now would be to skulk,
A gangster in the shadow.
It was at home here,
And anyway the energy it would take.
So many hours to let it out.

9.

When I died
I did not die,
I had not been as things are.
When I was remembered
I was remembered wrong.
It was a bargain circus act
When they placed the sheet
Over my hard-drawn face.
Underneath I vanished,
But crudely.
There was an after-image,
The sort a flashbulb leaves,
Worn pennies on my eyes,
A quiet lipstick,
The letter O spelled
By the legible graphite
Line of my lips.
People remembered me
Thereafter as someone else,
As if I had been afraid.

The Work of Remembering
Saint Louis

1.

Teodoro Luna lost a hand.
He could not recall
The circumstance of its separation:
One week it held bread to be buttered,
Then another week
In need of fingers
There were none.

Remembering anything now
Took enough of him,
So many small requirements
Of the night,
Covering Saint Louis
The jack-parrot, feeding
The neighbor dog
To take sadness from its eyes:
All of this explained
His missing hand.
A hand here, a tongue for the moment
Forgotten there,
Who of us, said Teodoro to his wife,
Has as luxury
The time to keep track.

2.

Teodoro Luna found his hand
Two months later
In a moment of surprise.
IIc had given it frooly
Supposing his act to be prayer.
He had left the hand fast
In his dream of the last houses,
At the end of the last
Line of trees in the world,
And he had declined in his sleep
To bring it back.

Finding himself
Asleep again, he found
The hand at its work:
A child's swing
Hung from a blue darkness.
His hand held the toy from movement.
No wonder, he thought,
He had given himself to this task.
There was no mystery here.

Passing Late in the Day's Afternoon a History

The Lunas took
From the moon
Its name
Seven generations ago:
That's the story
No one changes.
Before Luna our name was *dog*
Or *tree,* something
From this world.
But the Lunas did not all come from this world.
Half of them were animals.

In a north Sonora bar
On a fat neck Imuris night,
Night that is Day burned up there,

Night, which is still Day but dressed up like a cat burglar
In black,
Day so hard at its end
It still wants to take more from a man,
To rob him of anything he thinks he has.
Day which will not permit him into night.

And Night anyway is not such a good place here either.
Night, which is the color of a violin case from the Twenties,
A machine gun inside,
Night the color of Stalin's moustache,
And which goes along with the curve of it.
Night, Doroteo Arango's mouth,

What is left of Emiliano Zapata's eyes,
The socket of Obregon's missing arm.

And Twilight, should we talk about it?
The Apache dance of their joining here, Day hurling
Night to the ground, Night looking hurt,
Then enticing a friendly hand,
But pulling that hand with its body to the ground,
So that for the moment Night stands on top.

Well, all right, it was dark.
Hot with dirt-sand and dead creosote air,
Old Lázaro Dog, or Lázaro Tree,
Whatever his last name was then,
My great-grandfather on my parrot's side,
He was thirsty and full of the big itch,
If you know what itch I mean,
And carrying the day with him
Under his shirt and in his pants.

And the moon too in those days
Before fans and coolers, before ice
Used to take more time off,
Getting in fights or drunk
For days.
There was no real night yet,
Day owned everything,
And the moon was a new job.

And it happened like anyone knew it would:
The moon and Lázaro
Wanted the same chair
And the same woman,
So there was a scene,

The spittoon kicked over and a bottle broken.
This was before movies.
This was where movies came from.
Lázaro called the moon's mother
Some fly-by-night, some hot comet
Just passing through
And the moon turned red.
The men stood stiffer and cleared farther back.
The moon put its immense hands
On the table, which was cousin-like
To the moon in its shape.

You are a no-good
And I will show you. You are
A June beetle, and I will fly you
By a string.
The moon was much larger than Lázaro
Had thought, so much of it
Slumped drunk and lazy under the table.
As it got up, it kept getting up
Until it filled the room
And broke the boards of the walls.
It pushed into the sides
Of the adjoining buildings, the dry-good
And the new livery.

They circled each other
But the circle now was around the whole town,
And the walk was slow.
It gave Lázaro time to think,
And he had begun to sober.
Oh shit.

Well then, said the moon, so large now
Its hands were lost
And its legs could show of no support,
You will apologize and then you will die.

Just like that
Lázaro hurled himself in a fury
Toward the moon,
And reached it.
This was before rockets.
This is where rockets came from.
To this day you can see
What only he could do.

He did not win
But neither did he lose.
It's that way sometimes with things.
He did not steal away the moon's name
But neither did he come back
Named *dog,* or *tree.*

And people mistake the moon's name,
They still call it Luna.
But it's the name we remember it had,
When it used to come down.
Luna is what we used to call it.
No one knows what name it has now.
It is older and will sign no paper.
It pays in cash.
It tries to forget.

Lázaro Luna has not yet come back at all.
We see him trying sometimes
And we hear him.

We have letters from cousins
Who know for a fact he is anxious to return.
We imagine him as a rosebush
In his struggle.
But a backward rosebush,
One which has flowered first,
And its flower is the Moon,
Away from which he has built
Under the guise of a minor scaffolding
Project gone wild, stems
And branches, thorn
Streets and viscous trails,
Looking to reach and root in the earth,
Looking to let go of its moment,
The moon,
Of its flower quietly
Into the air.

Half Hour of August

1.

He could not breathe: the heat
In his left hand, her mouth
So placed
He dared not move: two
Panes of glass pressed together,
The chance of fire
In his hand:
It was her lips moving,
The lecture of physics,
Of particles moved to the side
And back around, the full
Lesson of stirring
A bees' nest with a stick.
He was unsure, he could not move,
There were not words,
He was afraid
But it was not the fear
For which the world is famous.

2.

The breast came off
Into his hand.
He had said nothing, had raised
No Sign of the Cross,
Not the gentle scapulars of his saint.
It simply fell
Of its own,

An act of disconsolation,
A gesture of weariness and of use.
As if to say, enough.

3.

It was not the first time.
Onto the river's water
Gone violet, away and warm
He sent the parts of her
She left
Through the years to his care,
The breasts, the legs,
The child worry fevers.
He sent them like boats on a river
Of desire: downstream
He imagined himself
As a boy, seeing his wish
For a woman suddenly
Drift ashore.
Or another man, collecting each part
As it arrived,
Building another woman from the water.

4.

In his lifetime his woman
Who was his women
Had come apart
So many times
He had stopped noticing.
Not that he was a bad man: simply
Because he owned no instruction;
Because he was not himself a woman;

When he helped put her back together,
He did a bad job,
One not of distraction,
Not the inattention of, say,
Eating an apple;
Rather, his was the fruit of inability:
The women he put back together were not
The one who had fallen.
Each had something of the other,
A familiar leg, a texture
Of skin unforgettable.

5.

Her breast fell
Into his hand
Which wanted it:
This other woman,
And another gravity,
So that her lips
Also fell to his
With certainty:
To have kept them apart
Having been a cheap invention.
So all their parts
In the snap of a finger's time
Gathered to themselves
Hard: for the moment
He was the circus
Man with four lips,
A man with breasts
And the legs of a horse,
He was the assembled
Hermaphrodite of school books

And the whispers of hallways.
It had been cruelty
Not to be so, exhaustion.

6.

No wonder she had felt
So tired in the mornings
And then again
In the late afternoons
For so many years.
It had not been desire at all
This whole time,
But remembrance:
It had always been like this,
And was again.
This was no risk of the new,
But the flatness of necessity,
An old fit.
How long they had held
Their breath
In this water of waiting,
How good to breathe
His hand again, or his
Ten hands,
Which was what it wanted
To be.

An Accounting of All Her Men

His eyes were once well set,
Forward aimed like any one of us,
But it is all deception now:
He sees only backward.
Each niece who has come
Looks like someone he has known,
Each stranger like a vendor
In the middle of his childhood
In the town where we met
And sometimes meet again.
There was a sweet air in those days,
Along the houses, in the valley
So many bougainvillea
The world was red.

I watched his eyes
Too much, and laughed our good laughs
For him. I did not see
This movement of his was no trick.
Other parts of him, his legs,
It seemed had lost their direction also,
But not for him:
He had not weakened. He grew stronger.
I had failed to notice how
For each ten steps forward
He took eleven strong ones back
As if he were a swing getting faster
Whose ropes were tethered to his head,
Tied in a fashion to his famous ears.

With that swinging walk
He walked himself
Backward into time.
When he walked
He did not get anywhere
But where he had been.
In this way he grew younger,
He grew impatient,
Then bold true to his days.
One afternoon
Slipping toward blue evening
He took eleven
Forward, twelve back,
A leap both ways
At the same time,
An arc beyond the compass
Frame of his legs,
Too much for a little boy,
And he tore himself in half.

That is why he says one thing
Then attends its enemy.
That is why he makes the sounds
Of all the orchestra with his face,
The woodwind of his nose, the brass
Of his needs, the percussion
His teeth make against the world.
That is how he is here
When he is away.
I will tell you something.
I meet with him now by remembering
Someplace along the reeds.
He will talk to me there,
In the way he used to.

His eyes have a covering, a silver
Closing of the head from disuse,
His eyes no longer finding adequate
The adjoining rooms given them.
Rather, the back of his head
Has cleared, become softer,
Almost hollowed.
It is there, I can tell
As I could when we were young
And he wanted to see my legs,
Into my red dress,
He cannot fool me,
It is there, at the back of his head,
His eyes are at their old work.